HOSTILE

HOSTILE

Heather Nagami

chax press 2005

ISBN 0-925904-53-8
Printed in the United States of America

Published by Chax Press
101 W. Sixth Street
Tucson, Arizona 85701-1000
USA

The cover of Hostile was designed by
Heather Nagami, Bryan Barnes, and Charles Alexander.

The cover painting is by Heather Nagami.

Thank you to the editors of the following journals where some of these poems appeared: *Xcp: Cross Cultural Poetics* (ed. Mark Nowak, contributing ed. Walter K. Lew) and *Antennae* (ed. Jesse Seldess).

Thank you to the following poets, teachers, friends, and organizations who've inspired, taught, and supported me: Charles Alexander, Charles Atkinson, Michael Blake, Sheila Brown, Peter Gizzi, Tim Peterson, POG, Sharon Reynolds, Boyer Rickel, Jesse Seldess, Ron Silliman, Roz Spafford, Kenneth Tanemura, and Amber West. Special thanks to Amber, Sharon, Jesse, and Suzette Duncan for their invaluable feedback on the final drafts of my manuscript.

Thanks also to the Caplan family for their incredible support.

Thank you to Dr. Geary for my life.

For my family

in appreciation of their support and understanding

In memory of my father, Koichi George Nagami (1938-1989)

and my grandmother, Ada Tsuyako Togawa (1916-2003)

contents

one

Acts of Translation

I. Figure 10.57. Hospital building north of Poston I.

"I was born in a hospital," she tells me, proudly (Figure 10.57), "driven out of the camp to a hospital" (Figure 10.57).

Looks more like a house. Horizontal wood slats, once painted white, now stained with water or fire, weather. Wooden porch with railings and wood slats sliding off. Garden hose hanging off side of wall.

Looks more like an old house in the South. Windows split horizontally in half, which lift with two hands. Screen door tilted, hanging on by hinge. Chevy parked crooked out back.

Still displays its distinctive double roof and other evidence of former use.

II. Figure 10.44. Relocation center hospital building at the site of the Poston staff housing area.

On the east side of the highway, the former staff housing area at Poston II now has churches, residences, and a relocation center hospital ward building moved from Poston I (Figure 10.44). The building, lacking its double roof but otherwise in fair condition…

"I remember each time I fill out a formal document, and have to write the place of my birth."

…currently being remodeled, is located behind the Poston Community Baptist Church. The church wants to replace or rehabilitate the structure. The ward building resembles a barracks, but is made of wood planks, not tarpaper.

"It was important to me that you be able to write, 'Newport Beach'".

Window frames, uneven, line the side, wood chipped, rough, scorched exterior. One building anchored outside of its original habitat, under gray sky, most likely blue, large, billowy static clouds, most likely moving, briskly, building in middle of, loose dirt, dried shrubs.

III. Figure 10.30. Classroom building at the Poston I elementary school.

Since no arrangements had been made, evacuees built their own classrooms.

"But mom didn't know if there was going to be one where we were going."

West of Blocks 19 and 30.

"So, she brought encyclopedias for us and for the other children."

Sufficient lumber was not available, so they leveled the ground.

"Only one suitcase, you know?"

The others brought bedding, toilet articles, eating utensils and clothing. Walls were created of adobe, a foreign material to most.

"You see how your grandma is? Even back then."

Mixed mud for bricks, lined hundreds to dry in 115-degree heat. Figure 10.13. Pouring foundation for school. Which still stands today.

IV. Daughter

Figure ten point. ten point. and they couldn't?

Intergenerational tension was also a major problem
in the relocation centers, especially since Issei and Nisei
were very distinct generations.

This book says, "Intergenerational tension was also a major… since Issei and Nisei were very… The majority of Issei leadership had… du da da dah… Pearl Harbor… Nisei gained power and… Once the…

However, use of the Japanese language was restricted: meetings… in English… publications… in English…"

Meetings. Meetings. And publications. What were. But then how did? I don't think this is…

But auntie spoke going in, didn't speak going out.

And you, born there, never spoke. Here it says, "meetings." What is "meetings"?

I don't think they let grandma speak to

speak to you, when you were born

speak "gohan"

speak

"hashi"

like you

spoke

to me

How did grandma

speak

How did

grandma

speak

how to distinguish shiokarai from karai?

What words, what, what, English? Shiokarai. Salty? Strong, biting taste, like shoyu? No, like, like, soy sauce, right? And karai is, is "hot", like, like, hot like wasab No, no, like, horseradish. Don't eat that. Hot, like horseradish.

V. Go

Go shih-shi
shi-shi, like water, like
shhhh, shhhh
sh, sh, sh

Go unko, like
ng, ng, have to go
unko, Mommy,
I have to go
Where is the benjo?
          ben, den, room   jo, O, hole
                    room with hole
Take the hashi,
          soft in your hands
ashi, ashhhi, ashhhi,
          cradle, lullaby
gohan and umeboshi
          in your hashi
    raise them toward your tongue
ashi, ashi

Ne-ne, ne-ne time
    lullaby, time to,
  time for ne-ne,
    shhhh, hhhh,
shhh, shhh,
    neh
        hhhh
            neh
                hhhh

                    Eat teddy-yaki
                              teddy
                    bear—furry   sweet—brown

squishy, fuzzy teriyaki kind, brown teddy bear

Wear your zooris
your zodies
one zody, two zodies
zodiac
6 mystical signs under each bare foot

atsui, be careful, atsui desu ne,
hot, hot ouch,
atsui, ot ou!

karai
kk, kk,
kut,
cut,

shiokarai
shoyu cut

VI. My name is

Watashi wa Tsuyako Togawa desu.

Watashi wa Toshiko Nagami desu.

Watashi wa Hezaa Nagami desu.

Watashi wa Hezaa desu.
My name is Heather.

Watashi wa Americajin desu.
I am American.

Watashi wa nikkei yonsei desu.
I am fourth generation of Japanese descent.

Doozo yoroshiku.
Nice to meet you.

Kore wa nan desu ka.
What is this?

Sore wa nan desu ka.
What is that?

Are wa nan desu ka.
What is that (over there)?

Ima nanji desu ka.
What time is it?

Sanji sanjuu-yonpun desu.
It's 3:34.

Kyoo wa nangatsu nannichi desu ka.
What is the date today?

Ju gatsu niju shichinichi desu. Kyoo wa watashi no tanjoobi desu.
It's October 27th. Today is my birthday.

My mother, Toshiko Edna Togawa, was born on October 22nd in Poston, Arizona.
She is sansei.

My grandmother, Tsuyako Ada Kajiwara was born in January, in Suisan, California.
She is nisei.

My great-grandmother, Tatsu, was born in YamaNAshi prefecture. No, I mean, YaMANashi ken, Japan.
She was issei, first generation.

VII. Yonsei

ichi, ni, san, shi, go

issei, nisei, sansei, shisei?

No.

Shi, which is a Chinese character, can mean "death".
So, we use yon—the Japanese number "four".

Yon-sei. You are yonsei.

Not death—say it.

Not death—yone, say.

say it:

VIII. Fourth Generation

white washed? banana? twinkie?

can't speak?

haven't been back?

Can't speak your own language?

own/ language?

oneesan of language

Why no Japanese school? Took it at a junior college? With all the hakujin anime freaks, martial-arts-lovin', Zen-worshippin', shy-Oriental-girl-fuckin', doomo arigato Mr. Roboto Japanaphiles?

Very brave you.

like kamikaze pilot

go for final dive.

Yes, Hezza san. Wax on,

wax off.

Wax on,

wax off.

Ganbatte!

Ganbatte!

IX. Ganbatte shikarishite

Ganbatte—like sand paper, harsh, tough
GHAN-ba-tte

shikatishite—like coastal waves—shhh shhh

ghhhh, shhhh

neh   neh

ghhhh   shhh

go neh

neh

ichi

ni

san

shhhhhhhhhhhh

Excerpts were taken from *Confinement and Ethnicity: An Overview of World War II Japanese American Relocation Sites*, by Jeffery F. Burton, Mary M. Farrell, Florence B. Lord, and Richard W. Lord. Tucson, AZ: Western Archeological and Conservation Center, 2000.

Table Notes

I remember the story of the ship that arrived in San Francisco Bay and was
rejected

Docked on the shores of Mexico
they walked toward a cross to beg help
The priest must have known they were Buddhists
but found them work in a panadería

"They ate too much bread," grandma says, a girlish smile
"and they got fired," she laughs

They walked north to California

Mom jokes, "Did you know your grandpa was a wetback?"

Papa used to talk about how he thought
they were going to win

After Pearl Harbor
that sure changed his attitude

We had the hotel then, you know?
One of the tenants tried to call me a Jap
I said, you're not pure American
You're not an Indian!

My mother was in Amachi
with Yoko and Auntie Nozawa
I'm glad Auntie Nozawa lived with them

We went to live with Akira's family
so we wouldn't get split up

They let me visit my father
at the hospital, escorted by
an MP—a woman

In Camp, we didn't have to pay
for anything. So, when we went
to a restaurant, I just started to walk out

The hakujin lady said, Hey!
you forgot to pay

Ruby was the girl who lived across from me
She worked at the Camp hospital. We were friends

I think Auntie Kimi was jealous
so she made friends with the girl across from her

Auntie Kimi was Kibei, so
she wasn't really Nisei

You know, "banana"?
That started *after* the war

They took over the barracks for Sundays

Kamisama wa teki o aise to moshimashita
(And God said to love our enemies)

They told us not to speak Japanese
But the Issei couldn't speak English

After camp, papa never went to church

Veinte cinco centavos para verduras para caldo
He worked in the market every day. The market
was his church—that's what the reverend said

"It was fun," Auntie Chiyo said, "because we didn't know why we were there
It was a time for families to be close

All the kids used to come over to talk to mom
She was in her 20's

But after Camp, when Pearl Harbor came up in class
I just wanted to cover my head. I felt
like I did something wrong

Kids didn't say a whole lot, just a slip
'Look, I killed a Jap!'

I went to a Catholic Church every day
Mass every Sunday. Everyone there was Mexican"

I remember the story of the Brooklyn and Ford.
After Pearl Harbor, grandma and grandpa lost the hotel
so when they got back from Camp, the brothers got together
and started the market

Now Ford is Caesar Chavez Blvd. The market
is run by a Korean family. Uncle John put off retirement
to teach them how to wake up early, get the produce fresh
—serano chiles, cilantro, tomatillos—
how to stuff the plastic bags
with corn husks, and dried red peppers

The Gift

after Kenneth Tanemura's poem, "Japanese For Busy People"

And I hear myself in yours, Tanemura-san. A line of questions that fall into
a couplet that bleeds into the next

whispered answers, brief, temporary, your hush barely brushing the soft hairs
in my ear, a hidden echo chamber

familiar to us. I never told you that my mother's father used to cry late at night
after Camp. My aunt

would hear his sob seeping under her bedroom door. *I always thought it was because he*
couldn't speak to us, his own

children, she told me. My mother said that he once took her to the movies
—James Dean and Natalie Wood. Even though he

could not understand, he sat with her, watched with her. Ken, I must confess
I did not know anata

before I read your poem, a gift of meaning, an understanding underneath our correspondence
concerning authenticity,

our arguments about essentialism, deconstructionism. Exoticize, Romanticize,
feminize—these are words we use

when we are not writing poetry, defining American standards of beauty as a fascination with
the untouchable. To own

another language, an American vision of a foreign culture—an assurance
of American normality,

possibly, a fear of Japanese normality, maybe. One can only sustain an obsession by
keeping it packaged,

distant. The Japanaphiles, businessmen, the young white men who fetishize
me and other women of Japanese descent

mimic our teachers' lips like we do. They might form their words more
accurately than us. I can't help

but feel a camaraderie between myself and them. I cannot help but fear this.
I do not know

if their motives are more or less noble than mine. I do not know if that is a question
for me to answer. If we ever decide

why we search for answers within a language that is not ours,
the journey will come

to an end. We learn a language that we fear we'll forget out of lack of people
to share it with. A language

must be practiced daily to remember. My grandfather did not cry in words, but wails
known to anyone, as mourning,

though he practiced this language alone. I cry sometimes for his solitude, but softly.
His wails, resonating in my ears,

reunite with the breath escaping my lips. Another fleeting answer: we salvage
the phrases spoken

by ghosts, a resurrection that may end in rest. Natsu-yasumi
may sound awkward here

except for how you describe it—summer of rest. Tanemura-san is an address I use
not out of formality

but out of commonality. We yearn to hear each other, find each other, to make
our sounds
so heard

that even the dead will hear us speak.

two

within this room

The black suit fit differently
deflated sleeves
a Bible on his side
His spirit somewhere   I can't here

I didn't cry except
if his wrists were deteriorating
for those who watched

When I turned around   I was trying hard
(the crowded temple
sobbing pews)

to think this is my dad.

parts of our house

i.
the doorframe separates the family room from the living room.

the kitchen table crumbles mold. kitchen table caught
a cold from daddy's irritated noise. mommy making jokes of him: a stand-in
separating family from the living room. our family is not living, he says.

ii.
family room heard no news of a wall crumpling in the living room.

the chair heard. what was mommy telling daddy? walls that earthquake-rocked
with. what was daddy telling mommy? walls that healed him unlike us. walls that
held him in for us. in the living room.

iii.
i heard the dying in the living room. i heard nothing.

the kitchen table turned. to the family room. and the doorframe aftershocked.
and the chair knocked the wall. but held to their positions. left him. in the living
room.

iv.
he lay crumpled.

the kitchen table walked through mommy's jokes of how the wall separates the
family. daddy has a cold. living the walls is like dying, he says.

The Secret

It was as if he were secretly more of a friend
to himself than to us, or to Mother. As if none
of us could be the one
to be at that time. He could pretend

for only so many years. He had regrets
piling up like heavy handkerchiefs:
one stack for myth
and one for truth. He'd often forget

the difference, apologize for not teaching
how to work a yoyo, though
I didn't care, I'd know
that he was somehow searching, somehow reaching

for something inside me I couldn't see, couldn't hear,
those words that would come easily today,
had he waited for today
had he tried to hold his secret just a few more years.

Reminder

In the mail   is a letter
do not open   she's my sister

In the room   is a woman
do not touch her   she's my mother

In the graveyard   is a tomb
do not love him   he's my father

She is sending   to another
in her twenties   she's a lover

She is clinging   under cover
wringing bed sheets   in her hands

He is hiding   he will hover
holding air   holding ash

Watch her creases   shedding fiber
like a mother   like a daughter

When you enter   she won't mention
that you love her   that you'll hold her

In this tomb   there is an entrance
if you find it   if you try it

Sestina for me and dad

Our cocker spaniel, Whitney, chewed dried plums
in wisteria
silhouettes and wind-blown seeds
as dad smoked his New Year's salmon.
Sunny portraits
like these hang

in my mind for hours. I would hang
on, sucking plums
that withered like wisteria
blossoms, shedding seeds
that drizzled over Whitney's salmon
belly. A fuzzy portrait,

she would pose for more. In hasty portraits,
she'd keep patient, hang
back like I did when pulsing plums
scattered molting wisteria
down. These hours were seeds
I'd capture. Her sloppy salmon

nose, the painted salmon
lining of her eyes–tangible portraits
that firmly hang–
ripened plums
perched like knots on wisteria
branches. I collected poppy seeds

from dinner rolls, built poppy seed
labyrinths that trapped the salmon
scent. A portrait
disarrayed: a father waiting to hang
his life with tea-green plum
flesh and bruised wisteria

bones, choked wisteria
roots–brittle as prune seeds,
tired as week-old salmon
leaves. I imagine my own portrait
where dad could hang
on to withering plums,

resurrect them to plum-blue blossoms: *wisteria.*
I scatter my seeds among the slapping salmon,
a tangible portrait for us to hang.

was because of

I can see you now
I can look up

someone who is not like a person
not like a father

You were more "Japanese".
You were more, more, more, and just more.

But what traits and why?
Where did you? Why are you, why are you? Was it because of?
Were you just?

If you had just, would you have? Would you?

If you were, would I never have? You were so much more.

If you never had, I would never have
and you would never have.

I would never have. Maybe, I would have.
Maybe I'd be still. Maybe I'd have been. Maybe I would have.

Maybe I never would have.

three

The Agenda

Roll Call

The new owner of a convenience store
on the southwest part of town
would like to keep the liquor license held by the previous owner;

he's gotten rid of the liqueurs and other quick fixes,
reducing the store's alcohol supply from four doors to three,
an accommodation that would be made only by a family man, such as himself,

especially considering the loss of profit—
alcohol sales being the main source of income
for such a small outfit, like cigarettes

at the Oriental and American Food store
on the corner of Grant and Stone,
not that it's a small place, but surely less populated

than Albertson's or Fry's,
and while his corner store brings customers,
there's gotta be that extra bottle to keep them on his corner instead of the one

two blocks down, which is exactly
what Council Member West has a problem with:
why does the neighborhood need another store selling liquor

when there already is one only two blocks east?
Council Member West thinks that the Mayor and all of the Council Members
should remember what happened when too many licenses were given on 4th Avenue.

Council Members Ronstadt and Anderson agree, and so does Ibarra,
who generally agrees with Leal, though Leal, the council member
for the ward in which the store is located, says nothing.

Juice, Council Member West commands,
peering down toward the man behind the mike. *I think you'll*
be surprised at how many people will be plenty happy with juice.

The Tale of the Substitute Motion

Council Member Ronstadt makes the motion that Council Member Ibarra replaces with a substitute motion; but Council Member Dunbar (new since the elections) asks Vice-Mayor West to address Ronstadt's motion, which, says West, has not been seconded, and Dunbar seconds, though it's too late to second it because Council Member Scott just seconded the substitute motion.

Open Hearing

Mr. Parker of 9564 Harrison Rd. does not desire a detour
for Old Spanish Trail, where he's biked since he was a schoolboy,

and Mrs. Brighton fears her safety—the proposed route
means an isolated ride: what if she gets a flat, or worse, attacked;

but Mr. Williamson of 9531 Harrison Rd. thinks Parker and Brighton are like his kids,
who must be protected and whose futures he must plan—

boulevards and department stores, not bike trails,
are the inevitable course of progress—this backward thinking

has got to go: the Trail was great when we were kids,
but now we need to let it go. Even though the Mayor cannot be here tonight,

make the tough decision, Vice-Mayor West:
a Target on Harrison and 22nd.

Correction on Page 4 of 10

On the third line down,
it's actually $1.4 million,
not $140 thousand.

City Manager Keene

City Manager Keene says raising taxes is the only way,
since the Council, ten years back, began a campaign
to deplete the City's reserves,

keeping themselves safe for re-election, scolded Council Member West,
who is not afraid to raise taxes, if it means
a much deserved salary-increase for City employees,
such as those in Solid Waste Management;

but Council Member Anderson would like to remind
all of the council members that a non-elected position,
such as Mr. Keene's, does not carry with it the responsibility
of answering to the people themselves,

who, Council Member Ibarra argues, must know
exactly where this new revenue will go,
before the council members can support the plan,

which, wrote the Tucson Weekly, is obviously just some
mindless concoction from a tax-crazy,
new City Manager,

a sentiment made perfectly clear during this study session
on a cardboard sign that a protestor raises up behind Mr. Keene's head:
RAISING TAXES IS A KEENE IDEA.

The Tale of the Misunderstood Motion

Council Member Ibarra wants to know if the Council just voted on what he and the audience protestors thought they voted on, and what Council Member Dunbar obviously thought they voted on (as we heard her scowl when she thought her microphone was off) and now what City Manager Keene says they did not vote on, though they will vote on it after a few months more of committee and community meetings, so what this vote did, really, was nothing.

Vice Mayor West at an Open Hearing

To audience (concerning Council Member Dunbar):
"Be patient! This is a new council member here, and she's trying to learn the procedures!"

To Council Member Scott:
"Your staff did not come to the meetings. They came to three, and that's it."

To audience:
"I listened to you. Now, you listen to me!"

Open Space

Council Member Ibarra wants to change
the Campaign Finance checkbox
to an Open Space checkbox
on the City's water bill.

Mr. Keene holds up a matted,
2 ½ foot replica
—same box, same place—
just labeled "Open Space,"

which Council Member
West takes issue with: "I remember
just a few years back when *you,*
Mr. Ibarra, refused

to let us raise the water bill.
And now, you ask for this?!"
to which Council Member
Leal responds (Council Member

Ibarra needs time to collect himself)
that the people can choose to check themselves
or not to check, and soon, Ibarra,
with sweaty forehead

brings himself
to make a motion
for a six-month trial run,
to which everyone says Aye
except for you know who.

Definition of Terms

Vice-Mayor West:
A Spanish interpreter for certain City Council meetings = customer service

Council Member Leal:
Spanish subtitles for all City Council meetings = a civil right

Let's Go Tucson

The Citizens' Transportation Advisory Committee,
the Tucson Public Transit System, and other City-funded
organizations, have been tossing around ideas to ease rush hour

—smaller busses to drive out-of-range residents
to the bigger busses, "continuous-flow" intersections
at Speedway and Campbell, and 22nd and Kino—

and City Manager Keene can be seen with an unusual smile
(unusual because he *is* smiling) on Channel 12, while promoting
a survey to tell the City "what *you* want. So, let's *go* Tucson,"

though some key options, like the much-discussed light rail system,
mysteriously enough, do not appear on the survey,
which Council Member Ibarra, not pictured in the commercial,

is quick to note during open hearing. Council Member Ibarra proposes
that Old Pueblo Trolley's plan, which includes the light rail system,
also be included on the May 2002 ballot, as an alternative to the City's plan;

but just as he requests this amendment, Council Member West, who also,
by the way, has recently become Vice Mayor, scrunches her eyebrows,
lifts her chin and declares, "The people have spoken.

The vast majority of the City's research committees believe the City's Plan is *the* plan.
Mr. Farrell's plan is divisive!" Amendment denied. "Divisive," Ibarra smirks while
turning toward Farrell and the other protestors, "Ms. West says 'divisive.' How ironic."

four

Dear Scully,

Unruhe: a Kodak Moment

the network switched our dates to Sunday nights—on my 20th birth
date—10-27-96—you point your Smith and Wesson 1076—
standard FBI weapon—at Gerry Schnauz—drywall sealer—

he stares you down—his nystagmic gaze—taps
on the cancer—unannounced—between your eyes—
(a mass—phobia)—you/
I do not believe

4-6-97—goddamn—it's a repeat—I know I've seen—but
you point your 1076 at Schnauz—I—compliment your looks—you're
duct-taped to his father's dentist chair—is it your hair?—your browlines?—he
pinpoints "You—are troubled"—have I been—Schnauz?

> in 8th grade—a boyfriend's touch is
> his exploration/ my tolerance
> then 10th grade—
> his abuse/ my shame
> freshman year of college—
> his desire/ not mine

a re-run/birth—I swear I've never seen you like—I've seen you every
Sunday night—could I—with this phobia—I—am—you—
you're beautiful—

I'll see you next Sunday—never again—like the last 20 years—
5 months—6 days—9 PM—Fox—channel 10

Never Again

i. window shopping

this weekend/ won't swim/
with my cousins on the 4th/ my legs/ my armpits
won't shed/ would they think I'm/ a freak/ I mean/ a dyke

how would I tell "Grandma/ I love women"
if only she knew/ the sincerity
astray from the eyes of men/ will
she think it dirty/ strange/ how I used to think

watching a woman/ watching a woman
repulsed me/ until I
watched a woman/ at the Nine
in feminine desire

I found/ a line/ will they/ be coming/ with me
will you/ can we go/ to get her

ii. in the Rye

you tell me—in our blood—is a hallucinogen
misinformation—breeding phobia
I need to control—that mark I've made—to state
my case—a remedy

coming out—set me up—the tools
were custom designed—the ink itself—
is defining—my nature

was bred—before I learned—
of fear—of power plays—
ink of oppression—of dominance
ink camouflaged—in blood

how do I know—who can I tell
are you one of me—one of them
should I—grab your forearm—
smack you 'cross the face
—wring your wrists—tear—you—break
you—throw you—hide you
wrap you in my sheets—
incinerate—this voice—tells me
I am other—this voice—your voice?—

asks—what pushed me to this—demands a
marriage—flowing, sweeping hair
and skirts—made-up—grins—feels sorry
for—such a hard life—do you believe
it's a choice—is it in-born—

take control—this is not—you—remind me—I have
an unannounced visitor—in mind—I'll burn off
this guest—for the sake of the rest

Small Potatoes

i. Monkeywoman

the Nine at midnight/ a special showing
ordered a child size Coke/ before "Silence of the
Lambs" wait for a shot/ wait/ for a girl/ for a/
because/ she resembles you/ or vice/ as rev/ erse

re/ hearsed my mouth/ ing 9 minutes/ a line/
"I'll have a" "Can I have a" "I'd like a"
"small" no "child" no "May I" mother
"May I have a child" no "some/ Coke?"

I think you/ in her/ "May I"
think/ in her/ you're not the type to
"May I"/ mother/ smile at/ you/ your smile
you're smiling/ for me?/ "and then some/
Sour Patch Kids, please?"

ii. "I'm seeing a different side of you"

when a counselor says "obsessive"
adjective/ condition

how can I tell/ how to read
try on   access/ deny
treat yourself/ program

conversations/ predicted
carefully/ a set up
they/ I don't say/ anything new?

I'd like the news/ what?
can't look you in the eye/
to tell you/ is my true fear/ ?

shall I strut into the Nine/ say,
"I've had the hots for you all year.
Let's go for a drink."/ I'm under age/
"How about coffee?"/ I don't do coffee/

driving me crazy/ dreaming/ bugs at night
thanks for listening

iii. Superstar

I've gained access/ this face
I got/ personality/ I see
as a woman/ I'll get to you
as a man

when I/ take on this/ face/
I/ recall/ my own   are you
my sister   mother
am I   your son   my   father
you   my partner   my   brother
are you   mine   lover

my strategy   on your couch
making faces   eye to eye   for this evening   a Superstar
I will pass   Scully   I will give

five

In the Awake and Asleep State

i.

You looked up to the left/ like you were going/ to sneeze/ You started to shake/ like this/ and fall to the side/ *I've just finished a sentence/ These men rush in/ ask my name/ where I live/* We caught you. We laid you/ on the floor and one of us/ got help/ *Why are you asking me these questions?/* We put your backpack under your head/ jacket over your torso/ *I didn't do anything wrong/* There are levels of help:/ *Where is/* to give help/ *my desk? Why does my right thigh/* call for help/ *hurt? And the arch of my/* tell someone to call for help/ *right foot?/* to look intensely worried/ You wanted to sit up/ so we put you in your chair/ *These men say I had a/* You didn't know your name/ but touched your wallet/ your backpack/ *No I didn't/* When the paramedics asked for your address/ *No/* you remembered the numbers/ just the numbers

ii.

in my left eye/ your face/

in my right eye/ the men rush in/

your face/ seconds ago/ was whole/ small

in my right eye/ they say/

you sat across the room/

they say/

But how many?/ how many seconds ago?

in my right eye/ they say/

Now I see only part of/ your face

the men rush in/

in my left eye

in my right/

so close/ But how far/

my right eye/ the men rush in/

how far have you traveled/
to arrive/ here/ and say/
you did

and whisper/

/No

/you did

iii.

Unenhanced/ axial/ CT images of the head were obtained from the base of the skull to the/vertex/ There are no prior studies available for comparison/

The brain/ parenchyma/ appears normal. There is no mass/ edema/ or hemorrhage seen/ Ventricular system/ appears normal without any evidence of/ hydrocephalus/ The sinuses and/ orbits/ are normal/

iv.

REPORT: This is a 16 digital channel EEG *Call Neurology* obtained following placement of electrodes according to *We don't have your records* the International 10/20 system. The total recording time was 42 minutes. When maximally alert, the background activity of this recording *Call your primary care physician* was characterized by posterior dominant 9-1/2 to 10-1/2 Hertz rhythm *I don't have a primary care physician* which attenuated appropriately to eye opening. The patient was noted *Call Campus Health* to be drowsy throughout much of the study *Where was it performed* and the EEG reflected this. Photic stimulation was performed *University Medical Center* that produced symmetric driving response. Hyperventilation *Call the University Medical Center* was not performed. The patient slept *They told me to call here* spontaneously during this study *They have your records* and adequate levels *They are your records* of stage II sleep *Call Records. You have the right, but you still need a doctor to interpret them* was observed. *Hello, Neurology?* This was characterized by *Who was the attending physician?* symmetric vertex activity, *Dr. Iserson* sleep spindles, *Did you come in through the ER?* POSTS *Yes* and K-complexes. *Dr. Iserson is not a Neurologist.* No epileptiform features *Who ordered it?* were seen either while awake *I don't know* or asleep. *Dr* Anderson *is a Neurologist.*

He should *be able to get the results for you.* This is a normal EEG both in the awake *He has an opening in 3 weeks* and asleep state.

v.

What hurt after you had it?/ Where/ (Breathe in deep)/ Which way did you fall/ (Now let it out/ In/ and out)/ Headaches?/ Spots/ floating in your eyes?/ (Look forward/ Keep looking/ forward)/

CT scan/ was negative/ (Is this cold or hot)/ EEG/ was negative/ (Am I pushing up or down/ I'm going to scrape my key against the bottom of your foot/ Good)/ Have you suddenly woken up somewhere and you didn't know how you got there/ Have you/ Anything/ Anything?

Well, déjà vu/

Hm?/

Yeah, every other day almost/

Do you pass out?/
(Breathe normally)

No/

(Blood pressure's good)

It's like/

(Just relax)

I was in my house/ talking to my friend/
Whoa/

(Under control)

and I thought I showed him/
my room before/ but it was the first time/
he'd been there/ where I grew up/
Whoa/ Sorry/

(It's under control/
Haven't been kicked in years)

Okay, well/ but he'd never been there/
I kept thinking back/ Maybe one of my
other friends came over/ to my
mom's house recently/ and I was
getting it mixed up/ but no/ I asked
my mom to make sure and/ no

Temporal lobe/ small seizures in your
temporal lobe/ possibly/ MRI/

Really?/

Seizures/ yes/ 3 months/ no driving/
authorization/ MRI/ appointment/ 6 weeks/

Hm/ Okay/ but/

You might have had a tendency that was
triggered/ Tegretal/ for 3 months/

3 months?/

or could be/ 3 years/
This may be/ /how it is/

six

Something Beautiful

for Elyssa

i.

The bananas have gone bad today.
The stylish head-bobbing cat's head bobs
today. The paper swan was a crane
when you made it. I can't tell if it
is day or night. It's 3:00.

ii.

The bananas really aren't bad
but I remember many times when
they have gone bad. It was that template
that tricked me as I spoke of it.
I fear that when I look at anything,
it will go bad. I fear if I count to ten slower
than you shut that door, the stylish cat will fall.

iii.

I imagine your paper crane fluttering
upwards, the sunrise on its wings.
Not really, but it sounds pretty. I wish
I could make things beautiful.

iv.

I hope you don't mind that I changed
your crane into a swan. It looked like
a penguin, so I turned it on its side
and folded its tail into a head.

I wonder if you really thought it looked like a crane.

v.

Lately, like last night, I can see
okay. I'll look around my house—
it looks messy, yes; but it doesn't look
ugly. It doesn't look like
"the dark depths of my soul."
It's a dirty house.

(Last night, I watched you sleep, your eyes,
closed, the ball of your
right foot twitched
and touched me lightly.)

vi.

Lately, I look at you and I think I love you.
I look at you and I love you.

vii.

You say my house isn't dirty. There are just piles of papers, books, magazines, and piles don't count. Why don't piles count?

viii.

When I used to think of bananas, I could taste
the under-ripe one that left my tongue
a dry sandpaper.

Today, you told me that you don't love bananas.
I thought only briefly—"bananas."

ix.

Your house is always clean. Not really;
but it seems so to me,

though you leave your underwear
on the bathroom rug
and use the plot of floor near your easel as a hamper.

seven

Schematics

Call attention to the concrete. Intuitively, we
understand and feel concrete.

Concrete can be constructed of data from any of the big
plastic machines at the movie theater where popcorn is made.
Grabbing popcorn out of the bag in the dark. Feeling salt
grind under your nails in the bag in the dark.
Go for specificity.
See the puff.
See the seed.

Zoom into a close-up. See the little ring on her little
finger like a little band of stars on her finger.

Render   Cinematic   Specificity

Does the form express your really true feeling?
Ask yourself, have I done something

sexy   irreverent   rebellious

Your concrete is inventing itself.
A sense of wholeness, integrity,
that feels true to you.
What shape appeals to you?

the hourglass, the cone, the Erlenmeyer flask

There is a kind of plastic surgery called otoplasty.
I think it's beautiful.
Look for specialized concrete that hasn't been employed before.

And lastly, be consistent within a certain formula

home + gun = safety

and other such givens.

The hallmark of an emerging form is coming.

Transformations *after Donna Haraway*

i.
transcends the boundaries of
(cultural)
a place a locator

like lateral
(nation) parts
or any other standard material

rejects parts
prime (viewpoint)
in diamond, ruby, quartz

entities, an ointment
(outdated)
for the anointed

prime example situated
(no party) would be
sitting, the wait understated

ii.

to be
acknowledged as a
or seen (body)

presents a
viewpoints by
creating a

for these to reside
though this place, this nation
in constant motion, it rides

iii.

on fluctuation
to be the ones to have bodies,
have bodies violated, in mutation

who have had to reclaim their bodies
renew their situation
history as a myth, embodied

by creating one location
(rejects the opposing views)
of any one nation

(combining the two)
presence that embodies, that is tangible
suggests that men would have bodies too

to be touchable
not hide (the body) on which their vision's image must depend
to be accountable

for making such amends
no party would be bodiless
no party would have the capacity to pretend

Ode to OCD

The counting of steps and folds of movie curtain,
letters of words that wander through your eyes
as I speak to you, try to communicate
through this wave of inspiration, this irresistible chatter.

The washing of hands and top of the freezer,
every last hair behind the bathroom faucet,
as I look for you, try to reach
you move the soap dish exactly in its place.

The voices that surface—doubts and threats:
"If the commercial ends before I blink ten times,
mother will die a gruesome death,
maybe by hanging, or by car."

Your eyelids flutter, frantic with guilt
from wishing it, from willing it with only a thought
that dares you to miss the cut just one time.

Wiping your face, you wipe it away,
with a peculiar arc of the hand that will only do the trick,
as I feel for your body, try to touch my fingers to your face,
you retreat into your wild refrain:

finding the middle, this endless search for balance,
after counting all the letters, you must find the one
that splits them in half. Split the words, split
the curtains, split the staircase, the traffic, the windows,
split the apples, split the woman down the middle.

Ritual

This is my home of trampled-on grass.
This is soil of wet black reeds,
rain of winters, oil of dew,
of rotting seeds, sometimes a slug
in the doorway. Walls seep
as caravans skirmish—flies, traffic ants,
ground beetles, gnats. My neighbors
hunt tightly between cement encrusted
in dried bulging weed, floor of crackling stones
and withered blossoms. I don't know why
you visit so often with your huge human eye,
narrow stalking eye. Peering through the side,
you choose this home, marked by mangled leaf fibers
and the last morning rain. You come and you leave
and you come again. Why bother with such a simple creature,
or so the others tell you—how they caught me in a jar once,
hopped, and scrubbed their arms as if they knew.
They mimicked and jeered my every move. But you,
you have reason to fear, your performance more accurate
than any other, more natural than you'd wish.
You know me like I know why the loose soil thins
trickling into crevices and deeper chambers, the winds
blow which way and how, I know where I'll be next time
you want a peek, to trap and grind me gently. Will I snap?
You fondle playfully, handle me skillfully in your fingertips,
rehearsing for the day you find the courage to let me know
that I am meager, lacking, I will never be enough.

Centuries *for Adrielle*

Your answer: a voice
I recognize. seas as salts
pour through pores,
volcanic, coral, industrial.

You'd say, B says
there are sides to a person,
we see only parts
in time. As if
they were the whole,
and different parts would be
contradictions. You haven't seen
all mine. One, two, I'd say,
green, black, purple, linen.

(May I
make you
a myriad?)

You are a voyager. Collage. Place. Process. Conception.
Signaling to the shore of the black, the white, pillar.
It echoes, returns repositioned. Warns. Enlightens spasmodically.

You make me
think (from myself).
Impressions so near
—my visions, as *I* see them—
are unmanageable, exhausting
in such three-day doses.

My question: to run
in moment with your voice. your tones. your depths. your rawness. stammers.
your clamor. linen. you're hidden. echoes. your cavities. caves. caverns.

Hero

Far to the North, where winter storms whip the weather-beaten coasts,
you feel a sense of satisfaction, a great greatness.
Your brown stringy hair whisping, curling at the ends.
Stoic glasses barely holding to your nose.

Staking your claim, arms bent, fists on hips,
you would like to be the statue of David,
but of course cannot let your right arm fall, nor shift
your left heel just a quarter-turn inward.
You don't even carry
the essential organ that makes young girls
stare with wide eyes,
wondering, if it's that small,
how does it get inside?

Your inside, under finely chiseled labia,
is dense, having never been dug out, and look,
though you cannot,
I will tell you that the skin hiding your pubic bone
is smooth,
not a hair in sight,

which is why I don't know why,
after rough winds notched my skin,
I returned to you that day,
clung to you that day,
also naked,
also breathing deep,
inflating my chest,
thinking it a rare and
splendid pose.

about the author

Heather Nagami received a B.A. in Literature/Creative Writing at the University of California, Santa Cruz, and an M.F.A. at University of Arizona, where she also taught poetry and edited *Sonora Review*. Her poems have appeared in *Antennae, Rattle,* and *Xcp: Cross-Cultural Poetics*. With her fiancé, Bryan, she runs *overhere press,* a small press that publishes hand-bound chapbooks with an emphasis on poets of color and other underrepresented peoples. This is her first book of poems.

recent and new books from chax press

Tenney Nathanson, *Erased Art* (New West Classics 5)

Caroline Koebel and Kyle Schlesinger, *Berlin Schablone*

Linh Dinh, *American Tatts*

Patrick Pritchett, *Burn: Doxology for Joan of Arc*

Jonathan Brannen, *Deaccessioned Landscapes*

David McAleavey, *Huge Haiku*

Norman Fischer, *Slowly but Dearly*

Keith Wilson, *Transcendental Studies* (New West Classics 4)

Beverly Dahlen, *A-Reading Spicer & 18 Sonnets* (New West Classics 3)

David Bromige, *As in T As in Tether* (New West Classics 2)

Nathaniel Tarn, *The Architextures* (New West Classics 1)

Nick Piombino, *Hegelian Honeymoon*

Jerome Rothenberg, *A Book of Concealments*

Bill Lavender, *While Sleeping*

Elizabeth Treadwell, *Chantry*

Allison Cobb, *Born Two*

Todd Baron, *TV Eye*

Karen Mac Cormack, *Implexures*

Pierre Bettencourt, *Fables*

Heather Thomas, *Resurrection Papers*

Nathaniel Mackey, *Four for Glenn*

Charles Bernstein, *Let's Just Say*

Hank Lazer, *Deathwatch for My Father*

Mark Weiss, *Figures: 32 Poems*

For additional titles please visit our web site: http://www.chax.org/

This and other projects by Chax Press are supported by the Tucson Pima Arts Council and by the Arizona Commission on the Arts with funding from the State of Arizona and the National Endowment for the Arts.

TUCSON PIMA
ARTS
COUNCIL

Arizona
Commission
on the Arts

NATIONAL
ENDOWMENT
FOR THE ARTS